Flexing Cactus

by Thomas Torrence

 www.trafford.com

North America & international
toll-free: 844-688-6899 (USA & Canada)
fax: 812 355 4082

Flexing Cactus

You can run but can't hide so close your eye's
and deep breath twice ....
....Don't let the sorrow
fright.

Flexfull Thouts

1. As Hector Villoso sit's and stairs's at the front of him, the north wall, he see's those pictures's of images of chaotic ways. In front of him he see's a purple rose and a fine mami chula, but within a face of a cheeta combined, with his feelings up high and thouts sifting   as he see's these images talking to him in A scince of his own guilt but somehow of beuity, but now it's far to deep.

   This mami cheeta like thing, stairs in his eye's his eye's are bright red simply becouse he barely blinks in that case there in A feeling of sand blast.

   Cheeta Chula – If you don't bury the cactus the cactus bury's you. And it will grow the rest or sarrow will also catch up and then the cactus will never rest.

   Hector wonders is that me it's mami talking two?
   he screams in his head, but never out loud only in his mind, simply becouse he will think he's haveing A haert attack, he nervusly paranoid when haert starts ponding loud.

   He can barely think for himself as in to him he feel's no more than brain dead.

   Hector – Bury the cactus, maybe but not always, I can blink in the right time around but I can blink when the water wash the sand away.

   Those rainbow dots surely makes me blink once or twice.

   And so on, Cheeta Chula's eye's roll's on to the back of her head then turn's compleatly green and she beams right into

4

hectors fragile eye's.

Cheeta Chula – your just like the rest of them, haha your
                  playtime.

Hector – what you mean?

Cheeta Chula – you know what I mean.
                  just look deeper in my eye's, come on it wont
                  hurt but maybe it will its up to you but if you
                  dont fine I'll make you maybe force you.

Hector – uhh why me?

Cheeta Chula – I didnt choose you, you choose me.

Hector – aghh uhh, how why

Cheeta Chula – hahaha, your play time.

As she say's it in a softly sexy way,

Cheeta Chula – maybe I should, piss on you and watch you
                  grow, your just like all the rest.

Hector – why, why cant I ever do something that will make me
            human just like you, are you human?

Cheeta Chula – you only could be human again if you wake
                  then maby we could playha ha.

Cheeta Chula – and you wonder whyhaha.

        Then she disappears into thin air.

2. In his mind he see's A fast glimps of A memory, but this

memory isn't normal to him, he feel's A deep surrounding feeling of sarrow comeing on to his emotions if it's rubbing on to his week spots and if it's rubbing on to his haert then this feeling then grabs on to his haert with A beutifull aztec princess pop's up out from nowhere, her with those deep black eye's she take's her right hand and grabs his haert and hit's hit raw, hector flexes as his muscle's get's tence and flex away.

That glimps of that princess fades away but it is now starting to haunt him, he soon wonders if he seen her befor?

And then as if he knows her, she come's back all drest up in her danza azteca and the big black deep eye's he remember's that face that beutifull aztec princess, she's comes out of nowhere, right in front of him and look into my eyes, and as hector does her eye's turn's   bright red, as hector looks deeper, he see's his second homeland mexico, and bang it all flushes awayinto the mighty sea as hector flexes hard enuff that almost pull a cramp.

Hector – nnoooooooo.

Why this happen why this happen why, why, whyyyy

3. As hector flexes his chest to the extream untel it hurts and turn's hard as A rock, his vain's start's to push out the skin, then A little white box pop's out of nowhere in the front of him and as he beams on at it, he see's his second homeland but this time it's A different scene. Mexico gets bomb'd from all the country's around the world, he gets A emotion of if they could only understand us more.

Hector then start's to urine in his pants, then the box disappers As hector break's down and cry's. tears start falling down hectors bloodshot, dry as sand eyes.

Meanwhile his freind jhonny comes up to the door, knok knok

Jhonny – ol' thats right he cant even get up.

Jhonny open's up the door and walk's on in, looks over to the south right corner see's hector, same place and same position like always from two years to now. hector silent like A cactus, with urine dripping down his upper leg's, followd by urine stain's from who knows how many times this has happened. And the smell of the apartment room of meldo and fungus smellin.

Jhonny walk's on up to hector and sits down five feet across , jhonny sits down indian style and wonders, when are these nurses gonna get rid of the vomi smell, well i guess I gotta do it myself.
Jhonny – dammm man, it stinks in here what hey did you piss your pants yep, dang looks like you did plenty of times and dont these nurses suppost to change your clothes and bath you. well I'll tell you what I will change your pants and the nurse will do the rest cuzz smell like I would'nt wanna say cool.

Jhonny gets up and start to walk to the north dresser desks and opens the top shelf as he see's two pairs of maverick jeans both same colure black, takes the one on the left it looks cleanr grbs it and go's back over to hector.

Jhonny – well i hope this will do becouse it bout all you got bro.

As jhonny starts to unbutton hector dickeys brown pant's hector start's to see wotlahx, A beast half buffalo and half lizard. Its head and face is A buffalo on down to it's back and rest of the body is A lizard with A human feture.

7

As jhonny start's to slowly unbutton hector's pant's hector start's getting tence thinking jhonny is wotlahx (woe-tuh-lox) and as start to talk in his mind and never out, followd by him starting to flex his chest.

Hector – knoooooooo

Jhonny – dang bro whats wrong man

Hector – knooooooooo noooooo

Jhonny then stop's

Jhonny – well if it's bothering you then cool I'll leave it up to your sister.

Hector then start's to loosen up and slowlycalm's down.

Jhonny – bro im surprised your chest an't cramp.

Hector rolls up his eye's and look up at jhonny after thinking wotlahx was getting ready to eat him alive and so on, as he looks at jhonny in fear, he see's those buffalo horn's of strength and those fearond eye's, and that thick raptile skin, wotlahx just ready to eat, and cloaw hector's flesh into littlebite sized pizza's but as his haertbeat slow's down wotlahx disapper's.

Hector – is that, no it cant be ....jhonny, I must be dreaming?

Jhonny – you'll alright man.

But lucky hector start's to feel that feeling that he does'nt understand, but when it come's on it always'make's him feel safe and sound when he was in any kind of trouble down the road in the past when he was well.

wotlahx is now gone and some people call this feeling personle power but to hector it has no name.

Hector's eyelids close witch is A miracle.

Jhonny – man your eye's look sand blasted I should A nurse to put eye drops are something dang there in bad shape.

4. Jhonny go's on and sit's back down, A memory comes to mind as hector slowly becoumes more relaxd.

Jhonny – hey bro ... remember that time me and you went downtime to crampsville park, here we are me and you stuck in texas dang it was hot, no water I think you was sitin by lugdush that freaky looking cactus all i know is at night it's spookyand I cant remember how we came up with that name. any way we seen salvisa and angel and dammmmm they look'd good I dont know what or where happend to them, havent seen them in forever but any you remember in tenth grade salvisa and angel was always stuck up only if we could ever get hook'd up wit them we could have it made bro.

Then they came up to us and started to chat wich surprised me as stuck up as they were.

Travisa – so what you two doing here.

Hector – just kickin it, watin for rex to pick us up.

Travisa – heheha

Angel – rex since when you start hanging around that
          nutworm.

Hector – since when you two stuck ups cared.

Angel – what ever.

Hector – so any way how long are you two gonna be here.

Travisa – why you wanna know.

Hector – well, ifigga maybe you two wanna go to A party at
       my bro house down by the border.

Travisa – it ant jose is it?

Hector – yahh you know him.

Angel – jose, come on travisa lets go.

Travisa – hold on angel.

Angel – hell nooo I an't gonna go over there, jose alway's
and every time has a party, everybody get's smash drunk and
no-one conrols themself, the people he hang's around the last
time I was over there was A big fight.

As jhonny's talkin to hector about the goot times.
Jhonny – yah bro ... angel was freaking out bout going to that
party over jose's haha.

As jhonny talk's on, hey bro ... I'll be back later on today or
tonight hmmm about seven pm or so ... ut I know you an't
going any where but hey I'll bring some chulitas taco's I
know you like them .... o .... thats right you cant eat those
dang, or I'll bring some chili soup or something I'll figga it
out later   peace out bro ...

A Stainful of Pain

1. As jhonny sit's down on the couch waghting for his name to
   be call'd in the patients room, he start's to hubut with his
   mind. goodtime's and badtime's, so and so's and so on's just
   hubut's and so on.
   The secretary call's his name.

Secretary – jhonny.

Jhonny – ummm hmm ..... o.

Jhonny – mmm o ...

Jhonny shake's in head twice left to right, and walk's over by
then behind the secretary fallowing her footstep's to Dr.
becker's office.

Dr. beker – jhonny come on in.

Jhonny walk's on in and take's a seet, open's his eyelid's
wide for A few second's follows by A deep breath in and out.
he sit's across mis beker, in A plastec hard chair.

Dr. beker – how have you been, how are you feeling?

Jhonny – bout the same, but then again it depends on my day
and mood even with medication I still feel mmm .. I guess A
little glazzi but in A calming way.

But it all was going good intell that brown cloud of sorrow
came raining down depresstion.
A memory stumbled in jhonny's mind something of itself
hurt more the memory. with it's on feeling, jhonny figer's he
might as well tell her if it hurt's that bad.

Sometime's I get this feeling bout once or twice A day, it's A little hard to understand but ... it might sound crazy, I figer it might make me feel batter leting it out so here it go's.

Jhonny – A dog I think A black lab something like thatbut any way this dog it seem's evrything is going ok for it, it seem's happy.

Dr. beker – the dog yes.

Jhonny – yah.

Dr. beker – did you had A black lab, is this the dog you had.

Jhonny – no, but it's the only way I can describe this inner pain feeling.

Dr. beker – ohh go on.

Jhonny – o yah, but any way. Then something seem's wrong but the dog doesn't know what it is, something just dont seem right.

It's owner calls it's name, red .... red come here red, and so red go to it's owners and so on they go outside to the owners truk, the owner mr pottad open's up the passenger's door then red jump's in then Mr. pottad get's on in the driver's side turn's it on and so on.

He Mr. pottad start's driving, on to A ally. Red dosn't know what's gon on, pottad get's to AN in the inner city, look's of A place where crackhead's hang out and dump's red out.

Now as red is out he looks over and see's Mr. potter driving off red wonder's now what, what did I do wrong, why ..... why ..... why it dont know what's going on.

As jhonny start's saying this his eye's becomes A little watery he hold's back the tear's.

Jhonny – red look's left to right thinking the pottad's gonna come back to pick him up. then next thing you no is the pet patrol comes and stop's they take red to the Animal pond pen, and so on.

Now that it is there, they put it in A two by two cage, about five minets later A nurse come's and gets him out as red fallow's her into A room, she then pick's him up and put's him on A table.

as red is wondering what now whats going on and so on.

The nurse pull's out A hypodermic needle and injects posion into him then red start's to feel it rushing up to his brain, once it does bam he's dead.

Jhonny – well that's the only way I can descibe this crazy feeling and emotion.

Jhonny takes A deep breath in and out to help calm him down.

Dr. beker – that does seem sad. or you sleeping ok

Jhonny – yes ... ok.

Dr. beker – Do you get these feeling's often, it sounds like manic depression.

Jhonny – Yes sometime's, about three or four time's A week.

Dr. beker – Well I'm gonna put you on xoputyern (x-oe-put-yih-ern) it's new, however it has some side effects such as sleeplessness and droseness.

Dr. beker – is that fine with you or do you want to stay on prozac just let me know.

Jhonny – mmmmh ok, I'll try it.

Dr. beker – I'll put you on 3.5M starting out, if it's bothering you any way let mek now.

Jhonny – ok.

Dr. beker – Here's the perscription and see you next week, fri/04/02 and take care goodbye.

Jhonny – ok bye.

Driplox Within

1. As he get's back to hector's apartment or more of A room, jhonny opens the door and walk's on in.

Jhonny – whaaaats up bro.

hector – uuuuuhhhm.

Jhonny walk's up to hector bout five feet from him and sit down indian style.

Jhonny – where was I .... o yah, I was talking bout the past.

As jhonny try's to remember the rest ouf the story something bad come's to mind A memory.

Travisa – So hector, befor us two queen's leave, and since you two loser's hit me up with your number and maybe I'll call you, maybe.

Hector – Ight   or well we dont have A phone, were poor.

Travisa – You an't got A phone .... ummm.

Hector – Look we are poor, we an't got what you got.

Travisa – We arn't rich.

Hector – Hey just come over to my place, it an't all that but A homes A home, it's only A five minet walk from your castle or home.

Travisa – Well maybe ... I dont know, if my dad will let me, he is strict too strict .... I'll might.

Hector – Just think about it .... kool

Travisa – Kool.

But then as everything seems fine, as jhonny remember's the dark side, that every memory hold's that glazzy cloud hit to mind.

Jhonny – yah bro I guess I must have forgot, those stupid cowboy's mest it all up for us.

As Hector, Jhonny, Travisa and Angel was all stainding by one to another, they start to see dust and sand bluring up in the air they look over and it's the randy brother's.
As the randy brother's draveing in that ruty black blazer jeep. They pull up to Hector and all.

The randy brother's drive's up, right in front of hector and jhonny, as travisa and angel moves to the right.

Jhonny – So hector, who you thinks all in there I cant see anything the window to tended.

Hector – All I see is tim and russ, the same randy brother's as always.

Tim on the driver's side turns the wheel to the left and drive's slowly, then stop's follow'd by now tim and hector see's face to face. Hector and jhonny walk's up to tim, tim givin hector and evil look while hector get's up to the window.

Hector – Sooo, what's up.

Tim – What's up, were looking for A mexican immigrant about 5'5" and A 154pds. You all haven't seen him around and o yahhe got's a few front teeth missing.

Angel – You to got problem's chaseing down old migrant's just becouse youclaim it's costing America too much, most of

16

them work.

Russ – Nobody asking for your opinion's.

Angel – this is America, I can say what I please.

But then as it was going halfway ok, Tim reiches down and pull's up A beer bottle.

Tim – Hey Jhonny.

Jhonny – What.

Tim throe's the bottle and it hit's jhonny right on the left side of the face.

Jhonny – aaauohhhhhh, you fuck.

Tim turns the wheel to the left and burn's out on to the road and leave's.

Angel – jhonny you alright.

Angel – Jhonny ....

Hector – You'll alrie bro ...

Jhonny – ummmmmm uhh ...

Angel – Jhonny you ok.

And there I was with blood dripping all down my face.

2. As jhonny is done talking about that smackup memory, He look's up at hector yet all this time he normaly talks with his head down and so on.
Hector start's to get and feel something horrible, A feeling of pain, in his mind he gets A glimp's of reality yet trip out on acid for so long, he reality can be frightning. Reality as in

look around you, people are killing in the name of god, or people may kill you simply for pitty reson's ...... Reality is nothing but A trip. but this reality that hector is in as he feel's he look's up at the cieling while light bolt's come crashing down more like A strobe light, and the room start's to turn witches green, that moldy colur with dark blue lazer's as if he was in prison, and wotlahx must have went and hide in some forest down by some river, and next thing you know A brown cloud start's to rain yellow dropas.

This is more or less just another flashback for hector about five time's A week.

Only choice hector has to defend himself from this andross is to flex, flex away this pain and sarrow's just A emotional junkyard just flex ..... flex .... flex .... flex away. The pain.

Jhonny – Hey bro. Im bouts to go to sleep, I'll talk to you tomarrow and hopefully that nurse will be here to change and bath you, I hate to say it but you stink.

Jhonny gets up and walks over to the old wooden dresser, then lays down and crashes out, but then he start's to wonder .... I remember that mayan medison man, I think its hector's uncle, yah fresno .... that's it, maybe he can help hector, after all he is A medison man, well it dont hurt to try.

Jhonny wake's up, he gets up and stand's. He then looks down at his wristwatch and it is 7:53.

Jhonny – Well, If im gonna go down to fresno's then I bettah get to the bus stop.

As he gets out of the apartment to out side he start's wondering.

Jhonny – I think I remember what his house looks like, it's blue and about yeh high, with A mexican flag in the living room window and o yah its dirty as hell.

He then get's to the corner, waiting for the star bus, A few second's later it finally arive's, as he get's on and gives three bucks to 8th street just a few blocks up. he walks on back and takes a seat.

3. Jhonny gets there and tell's the driver to stop, and so the driver does He then gets off, he look's over to the right of him and doesn't see it, he then look's to the left and there it is on top of thehill, he quikly run's up to and up to the door, KNOCK KNOK.

Fresno – who's there.

Jhonny – it's me jhonny.

Fresno – Who.

Jhonny – Jhonny.

Fresno – hold on.

Fresno open's up the door, first stumble'd by who it was.

Fresno – Jhonny, dam your big and you look diffrent.

Jhonny – yah, I gang'd A little bit of waght.

Fresno – Well come on in man.

Jhonny – OK, dang bro ... you'll looking like some kind of santana are something.

Fresno – hahha ..... well take A seat somewhere.

Jhonny goe's on and sit's on the cautch on the right from him as fresno sit's on the chair left from jhonny.

A Flexible Shame

1. Meanwhile as jhonny's over fresno's seeing if maybe hector
   can get cure'd, Hector's sister Florisa comes over to hector's
   apartment room and opens the door and so on.

   Florisa – HECTOR (she say's out loud), hector it's me your
   sister, I got some chicken noodle soup for you.

   But then something doesn't seem right for hector, he start's to
   get tence follow'd by his chest flex to the max, his sister
   look's at him and wonders what is wrong? As his sister walks
   up to hector, hector's eyelids open's wide as he start's to
   shake and next thing you know his sister turn's into
   WOTLAHX.

   Florisa – Hector you alright.

   Hector – uhhhh ummmgh.

   Hector I cant take this anymore, He pull's his right arm up
   with his thump out and up, and pops out his right eye.

   Florisa – NNNOOOOOOOOOOO.

   Florisa quikly runs out and to next door at the neighbor's, the
   venbedas, she knoks hardly as Mr. venbedas open the door.

   Mr. Venbedas – What ... what.

   Florisa – Please call the ambulance.

   Mr. venbedas – Why ....

   Florisa – Quikly now.

Mr. venbedas – Alright .... alright.

And ten minutes later they arrive and take him to cleraz hospital and so on.

2. And so on's at fresno's.

Fresno – So how can I help you and what's up.

Jhonny – Hey bro it's hector ... he's ... well he tript ou man.

Jhonny – You are A medicine man, can you help hector.

Fresno – Well ...... maybe.

Jhonny – I hope so, hector's like A brother to me.

Fresno – Hmmmmmm ... I might, In this case it will be hard but maybe.

Fresno – Well hold on ok.

Fresno gets up and walk's into the back room and ten minuts later comes back to jhonny and gives jhonny A black leather pouch. inside it, is A mixture of erbs with A funky smell.

Fresno – take this and put it in hector's left hand.

Jhonny – O .... OK, well goodbye and thank you bro.

Fresno – Peace out man.

3. Jhonny ofter gitting the cure go's back to the bus stop waiting for the ride.
The bus finally come's and picks him up.

Finally jhonny gets back over to hector's apartment.

Jhonny – Whohuaaaaaa ... wheres hector, mmmmmmmm. I
betta call his sister they might have took him away
or something.

Jhonny gets out and walks to A payphone, he then call's
hector's sister picks it up.

Florisa – Hallo.

Jhonny – Hector isnt over his place, you what happnd to him.
Im kinda worried.

Florisa – Jhonny immmmmm, I'm sorry. but something bad
happend.

Jhonny – What, what.

Florisa – Well, just go to room 22, 1st floor at dredville
Hospital.

Jhonny – Mmmmm, OK.

Jhonny gets to room 22, he then walk's on in and see's hector
sleeping flat on his back with his right eye all banded up.

Jhonny – Man bro .... What happened to you!

Jhonny then remembers the little black pouch and then pull's
it out from the right side of his blue jeans and puts it in
hector's left hand, and the next thing you know Fresno pops
up right behind jhonny.

Jhonny – Fresno ... Man you freak'd me out bro ...

Fresno – HAHAHAHAHAA ..... It's cool, so how is hector
          doing.

Jhonny – Mmmmmm ... Not to good but he is sleeping right
          now.

Fresno – Well .. I hope this works.

Fresno walks in front of jhonny to hector and put's both of
his on top of hector's chest, both of fresno's thumps right in
the middle of hectors heart.

Fresno – O Great Mother heal this man's weak heart and
          mind.

He then takes his right hand and go's into his blue jean jacket
and pulls out A little clear crystal and places it on top of
hector's heart in the middle.

Fresno – With the power of Great Mother, I heal your sickness
          and so begone.

All of hectors pain, sorrow and inner problem's turn into A
little black cloud and go's out of his noise like smoke and on
down to the clear crystal and magicly go's in the crystal like
water as it become's it.
The crystal is now black as black.

Fresno then removes it and slams it on the ground, it shatter's
like glass.

hector wakes up while jhonny and fresno smile from releafe.

Hector – Maaaaaannnnn ... What happend, OOOUUCHH my
eye.

Fresno – Yeesss, it work'd.

Jhonny – How you feeling.

Fresno – Well I must leave now but you two come over
sometime.

Jhonny – O'l I will.

Fresno – Peace out.

Hector – Mmmmm man, what happend to my eye.

Jhonny – I can't say, but all I know is tiz along story.

Hector, what you mean.

Jhonny – Just A long bad trip.